Coaching the Inside Veer

By: David Weitz

All Right Reserved
© 2016 David Weitz

Table of Contents

I. Overview
II. Count System
III. Quarterback
IV. Dive Back (B Back)
V. Pitch Back (A Back)
VI. Wide Receiver Blocking in the Inside Veer
VII. Offensive Line
VIII. Tags
IX. Play Action from the Inside Veer
X. Group Drills
    a. A Frame
    b. Mesh
    c. Outside Option
    d. Pods

Find more information and books from Clean Coaching at CleanCoachingBlog.Wordpress.com

Overview

The Inside Veer is one of football's most dangerous plays. It is an offensive system within one play that can result in three different players attacking three different zones depending on the defense's response. In addition, the Inside Veer is a versatile play that, while normally run from Under Center, can be quickly adapted and run from Shotgun for added variety. The Inside Veer takes a significant amount of time to practice but once mastered can lead to massive gains.

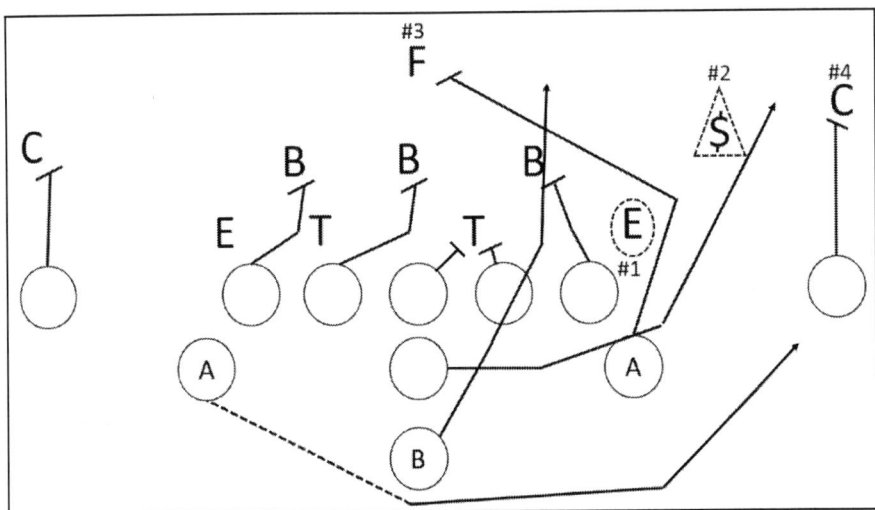

The Inside Veer vs. an Even Front Single High Safety look

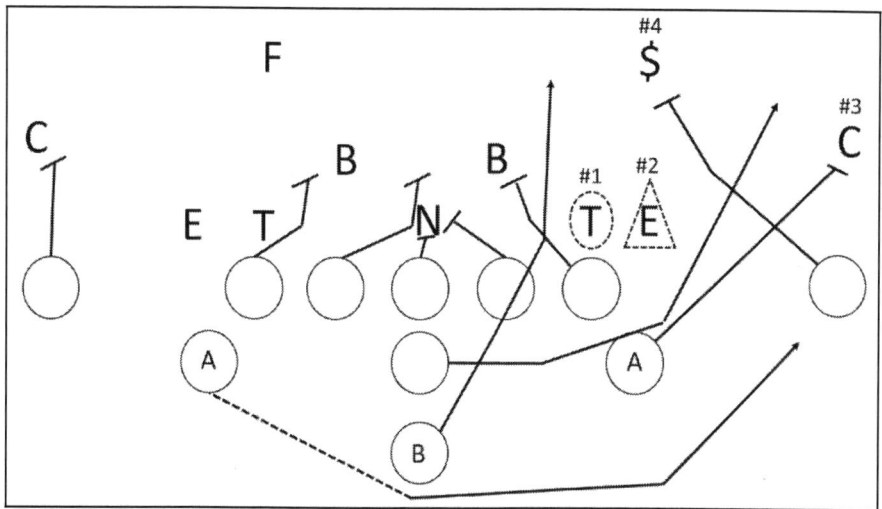

The Inside Veer vs. an Odd Front Two High Safety look

The general idea of the play is that the ball will end up in the hands of either the dive back, the quarterback or the pitch back, depending on the reaction of the dive key and the pitch key. What makes the Inside Veer so deadly is that each of the three attacking option are designed to attack the defense in three different areas. The dive back is running directly off the guard, through the B gap. If he gets the ball he can get into the defensive backfield in a hurry and gain yardage very quickly. If the Quarterback keeps the ball he is attacking Off Tackle and can clear the primary run defenders in a hurry and get to open space. When the pitch back gets the ball he will more than likely be gaining huge amounts of yards since he is getting the ball in space on the outside. Normally this is one of the offense's quicker players so by giving him the ball in space he can break a play for a touchdown very easily.

Count System

The Inside Veer is a play that requires the whole offense to be on the same page. This means that they must all identify the dive key, pitch key, flat defender and near deep defender. Once these players are identified each player will know their responsibility.

The best way to simplify this system is by using a counting method and giving the defensive players numbers. This numbering system works from the inside out starting at the dive key and ending at the near deep defender. This means that #1 is the dive key. This is the first player on the line past the B gap, this player will be unblocked and the QB will read him to determine if he should give the ball to the B Back or keep it. The next player in the count is the pitch key or #2. This is the player that the QB will read to determine if he should pitch the ball to the A Back. #2 is identified as the next player outside or behind #1.

As the count progresses into the secondary #3 and #4 are identified. These two can be identified together because #3 is the force defender who will be responsible for the D gap and will more than likely take the pitch man. #4 is the player who is responsible for the deep section of the field, many times this is called the Near Deep Defender.

It's important that the whole offense is able to identify all players within the count. This is critical because it means that the whole team is reading the defense the same and will ensure that the correct players are left unblocked. This can be done very easily using film study. When players understand the system for counting the defense they are not forced to memorize their assignment and can rely on the counting system to identify their responsibility.

What helps in identifying the role of a player is by viewing them as pairs that work together. Assuming the defense is sound #1 and #2 will be close to each other somewhere around the Playside Tackle. When looking at the players as a pair it's easy to find hints about their assignments based on their stance and alignment. This same concept works for #3 and #4. Whichever defender is the Near Deep Defender, #4, will have to be playing back quite a ways to protect himself getting beat deep. This normally leaves only one player on that side, the left over player is #3.

Quarterback

The Inside Veer is dependent on the ability of the Quarterback. Due to the speed of the play the quarterback has no time for thinking during the play. This means that he must have worked on the play enough in practice that his reactions are instincts. When the quarterback has worked both his footwork and mesh reads enough that he can make the correct reads without thinking he is ready to run the play.

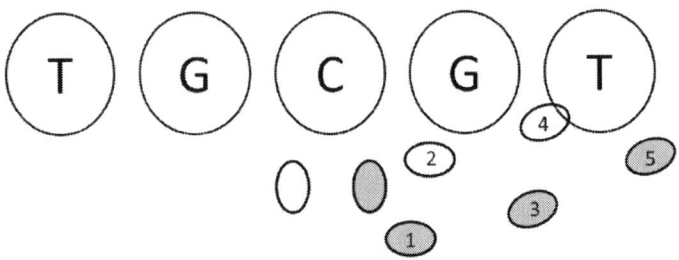

Quarterback's Footwork for Inside Veer

The quarterback's first responsibility is to get the ball to the mesh point quickly. He must do this by taking the first step with his play side foot. There are two main ways to teach the quarterback footwork for Inside Veer. The first way to teach the quarterback his footwork is having him imagine he is standing at the 12 of a large clock. If you are using the clock method you would tell the quarterback to step at 4 o'clock with his first step and 2 o'clock with his second step. This would put him at the mesh point.

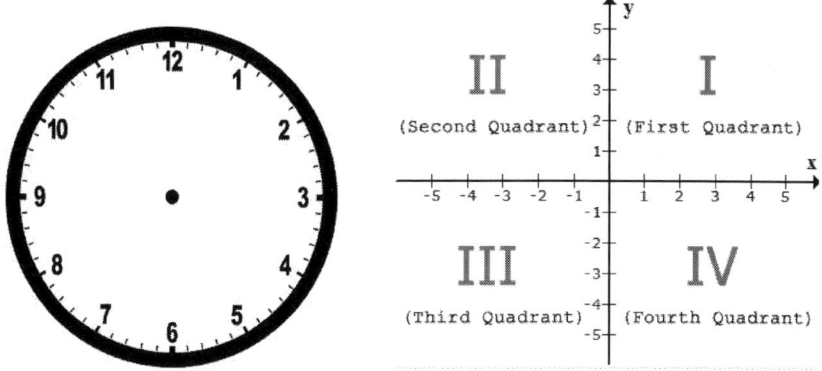

The second way of teaching footwork is to use the quadrant method from geometry. Using this method you tell the quarterback to step into quadrant four with his first step and quadrant one with his second step.

Regardless of the method the quarterback should be in the Pre-Mesh Position with his feet parallel to the dive back's path, his knees bent in an athletic position, the ball stretched back and his eyes on the dive key.

This play requires excellent decision making by the quarterback as his split second decisions will determine who gets the ball and if it will result in a big play or a turnover. For the dive back he will be reading #1 or the first player outside of the B gap. The process of reading the dive key is called reading the mesh.

In order to make this an easier read the Quarterback is told to give the ball to the dive back every time unless the dive key can tackle the Running Back for less than four yards. If the quarterback thinks the dive key will tackle the running back he will keep the ball and attack the pitch key.

When facing the pitch key the quarterback should be thinking "keep the ball every time unless the pitch key can tackle him for less than four yards." If the QB thinks the pitch key is not honoring him as a runner and he can gain four yards he will plant his foot and get up field. If the pitch key attacks him he will pitch the ball to the pitch back by turning his thumb down and stepping towards the pitch key with his play side foot. He will finish the pitch by stepping with his backside foot to the pitch key. This closes his hips from the defender which softens the potential hit he may receive.

The Inside Veer is very dependent on the Quarterback reading the mesh. Many teams that run the Inside Veer will spend up to 20 minutes a practice working through the Quarterbacks reads. For more information on teaching the Quarterback to read the mesh check out my E-Book "Coaching the Quarterback Mesh."

Dive Back (B Back)

The role of the B Back is one of the most under coached parts on the Inside Veer. It's very easy to tell him to get to the mesh and run hard when he gets the ball. While these are the two most important parts of the B Back's job there are many subtle coaching points that can turn a 4 yard gain into a touchdown.

The aiming point for the B Back on the Inside Veer play can vary slightly. Some teams will have him aim straight down the middle of the Guard while others will have him aim directly for the B gap. Like anything the best aiming point depends on the players running the play but an aiming point of the outside foot of the PSG is a very good base to start from. This aiming point allows him to get wide enough where the Guard can have a stale-mate without ruining the play. At the same time by aiming at the outside leg of the PSG he is tight enough to force the dive key to come down hard in order to make a tackle which makes the QB's read much easier. It's important that to find a B Back who is able to run through arm tackles.

Due to the speed of the play the B Back's footwork is crucial. He must start the play by taking a step with his play side foot directly at the PSG's outside foot. It's important that he explodes low and fast to force the dive key to make a choice. While the PSG's outside foot is his aiming point the B Back must remember he is responsible for getting his belly over the ball. The quarterback will have some slight variations from time to time and the placement of the ball will vary slightly. It's the B Back's job to secure the mesh by running over the ball. By doing so he allows the Quarterback to read the Dive Key.

As the B Back gets to the mesh he should arrive with a big pocket with his eyes reading the playside blocks from the Tackle and Guard. One habit that many young B Backs have is to reach for the ball instead of letting it reach their stomach. In the mesh the B Back's stomach acts as a third hand to help secure the ball. By reaching for the ball it not only messes with the QB's give/pull read but also decreases ball security.

As the ball reaches his pocket he will fold his arms and shoulders over the ball to hide it from any defender, his control of the ball must be firm enough to control the ball but gentle enough to allow the QB to pull the ball out if he needs to.

After the B Back disconnects from the mesh his job is not done. It's important that he continues to run with his shoulders over his knees to hide if he has the ball or not. He wants to hug tight to the PSG and PST's blocks and ride the wall up to the secondary level. Once the fullback gets past the initial defenders he should get up field to gain as many yards as possible.

The B Back's reaction if he does not get the ball is critical to the play and, if done correctly, can open up space for the Quarterback and pitch back. The number one rule for the B Back if he doesn't get the ball is that he never cuts to the play side. By cutting to the play side he will take any defenders that might think he has the ball towards the quarterback or pitch back. The B Back should maintain his path and cut back away from the pitch back and quarterback. This will bring any defender who is watching him away from where the ball is going. Sometimes this will be an outside linebacker or a secondary player who has fallen off his responsibility and become concerned with stopping the B Back other times this will be a backside player who is running a pursuit angle. Either way this simple cut can put as many as 3 players in a bad position to tackle the QB and pitch back.

The B Back plays a huge role on Inside Veer. While it's very easy to not really coach him and focus on the Quarterback and Pitch Back, in order to get true explosion from the play there must have a B Back who is doing his job even when he is not getting the ball.

Pitch Back (A Backs)

The pitch back on the Inside Veer play is a key part of the play. He is responsible for forcing the defense to cover all the way to the sideline. Many defenses will focus on the dive back and quarterback in an effort to stop the two main players in the option. An explosive pitch back can punish them with explosive, long runs. The nature of the play is that when the pitch back does get the ball it should be a big play, because of this, many defenders sub-consciously over play the pitch back if he has an effective run or two. This causes the interior running lanes to open up.

One of the best parts of the Inside Veer play is the ability to run it from multiple formations and looks. While the standard formation to run it from is the flexbone it can easily be adapted to be run from a Spread (2 WRs each side), Pro I (two RBs behind QB and a TE) or any other formation imaginable. The thing that allows this to happen is the motion of the pitch back.

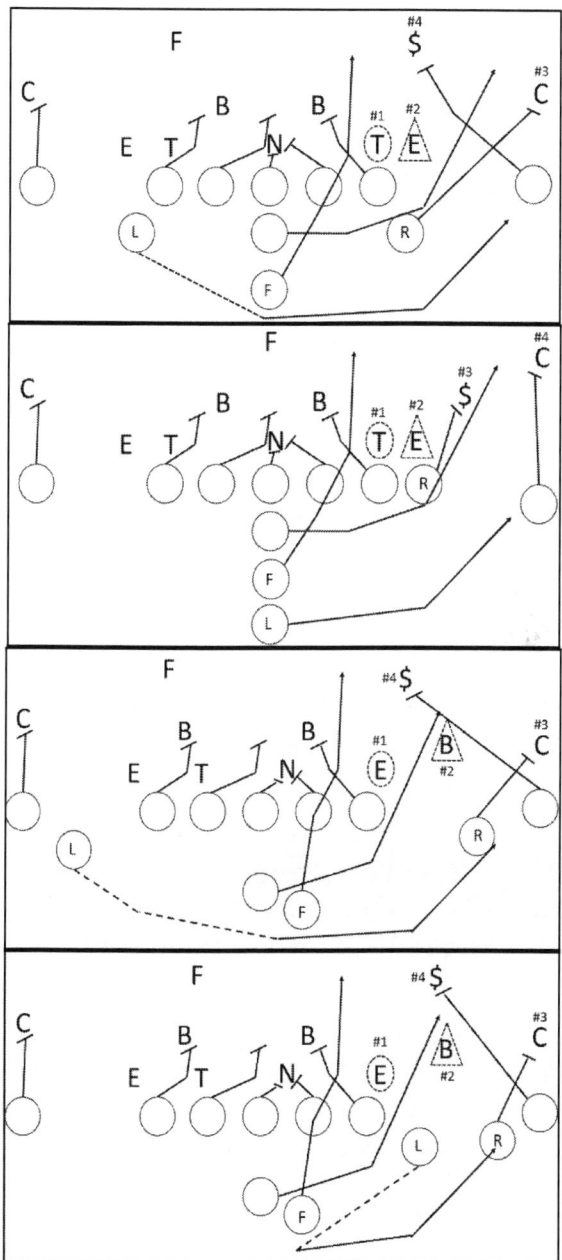

The above play diagrams show how it is easy to run the Inside Veer from multiple formations and player's responsibilities remain the same (using the count system)

The pitch back is responsible for being in a great pitch relationship immediately after the QB disconnects from the mesh. He must be in this position by the time the QB finishes his mesh in case the defense runs a blood stunt and the QB is forced to pitch right away. The best way to get this point across is to tell the players that it is their responsibility to get into this position, it doesn't matter when they have to leave but they need to be in that position as soon as the QB comes off the mesh.

While there is some flexibility with when they leave, there is no negotiation for the speed of their motion. When they go in motion it must be a fast motion. Nothing forces a defense to adjust like a quick motion. If the motion man is moving slow it puts no pressure on the defense and they can easily adjust. If the defense can adjust easily the offense loses all advantage of putting a man in motion.

The pitch back must get into a great pitch relationship. While the exact definition of a perfect pitch relationship can vary from coach to coach, there is one rule that applies to any pitch relationship: the pitch key can't be able to tackle both the QB and the pitch back. As long as this rule is followed, and the pitch back is behind the QB, the pitch relationship is successful. This is a skill set that requires that the pitch back and quarterback work together and develop a chemistry. In time they will find the pitch relationship that works best for them. It's easy to over coach this relationship but with time and reps they will find what works best for them.

Some coaches have moved towards teaching their quarterbacks to pitch the ball based on the leverage they have on the pitch key. The idea is that if the pitch key cannot tackle the pitch man the QB should pitch it right away. This is a way to get the ball out on the sideline quicker. It can be a very effective way to stress the defense and get the ball in the hands of a playmaker in space.

When the pitch man does receive a pitch he should be thinking big play. By this time the dive and QB run portion of the option have already been accounted for by at least two defenders. This allows the pitch back to get to the edge of the defense. Here he can use his speed and accelerate away from any defenders who are pursuing him. By getting to the edge he not only allows himself to get more yards but he also will force the defensive secondary to worry about covering all the way to the sideline on future plays. If the safety is worried about covering to the sideline this will give the Fullback and quarterback a chance to cut underneath him and create a big play.

Wide Receiver Blocking in the Inside Veer

While the line does the majority of the blocking in Inside Veer the role of the Wide Receiver in creating a big play cannot be emphasized enough. The best way to sell Wide Receivers on the importance of their block is by calling a successful downfield block exactly what it is, a Touchdown block. Many times if the Wide Receiver is able to make his block he will spring the ball carrier for a touchdown. It's important to call this out during film sessions and give credit when the receiver does a good job with their block. By being an effective downfield blocking team the receivers also open up the play action pass which can be a deadly component of the Inside Veer.

In a traditional Inside Veer scheme the Wide Receiver is responsible for blocking the Near Deep Defender or #4 in the Counting System. This means his job is to block the defender who is covering the deep part of the field on the play side. This can vary depending on the coverage the defense is running. For example, in Cover Two the Safety is the Near Deep Defender while in a Cover Three look it's the Cornerback. It's important that the Wide Receiver gets enough reps to recognize who is responsible for the deep section of the field.

The best way to teach receivers to identify the Near Deep Defender is to have them look at the play side safety before the play. If the safety is moving down or has a posture that indicates that he will be playing the flat the Wide Receiver knows that he will be blocking the Cornerback. If the Safety is sitting back and has a posture that he is not coming down the Wide Receiver knows that he will more than likely be blocking him. This is a skill that must be practiced but, when combined with film study many receivers can pick the correct Near Deep Defender over 90% of the time.

If the Wide Receiver has seen that the Cornerback is the Near Deep Defender he must take the correct steps to block him. One rule for the Wide Receiver to remember is that his goal is to block the defender for the least amount of time necessary. He doesn't need to block his man for the whole play, he only needs to block him for a second. But that block at the crucial time can spring the runner for a touchdown.

One of the best ways to shorten the time the receiver needs to block is to get the defender to retreat off the ball. This can be accomplished by playing into his coverage responsibility. If the Receiver takes a release that threatens the Cornerback's deep leverage the cornerback will be forced to back pedal and stay deep. This lets the receiver buy time and set up a great angle so that when the defender does come up to defend the run the receiver is in a position to keep him from making the tackle by walling him to the outside or inside.

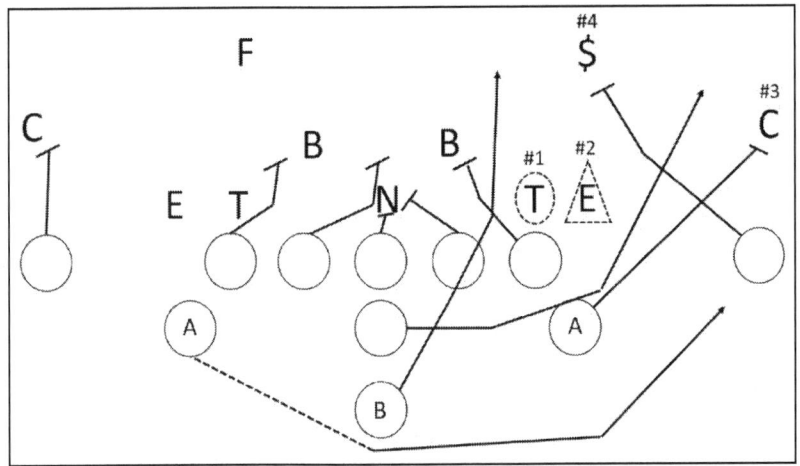

Blocking the Safety as the Near Deep defender is a little bit of a different angle but many of the same principles apply. In this case the Wide Receiver needs to take an inside release to get into position to make a block immediately. When the Wide Receiver is responsible for blocking the Cornerback he doesn't have to worry about the Cornerback tackling the dive back.

If the Wide Receiver is responsible for the Safety he must be able to prevent that Safety from tackling the dive back. This forces him to get inside immediately to gain leverage on the Safety. While the departure angle is different many of the same rules apply. The receiver doesn't need to have a block that lasts for 10 seconds, instead he only needs to block the safety enough that he can't make play on the ball carrier. This means that his block might only be for a second or two, but if he can maintain the correct leverage he can spring the runner for a touchdown.

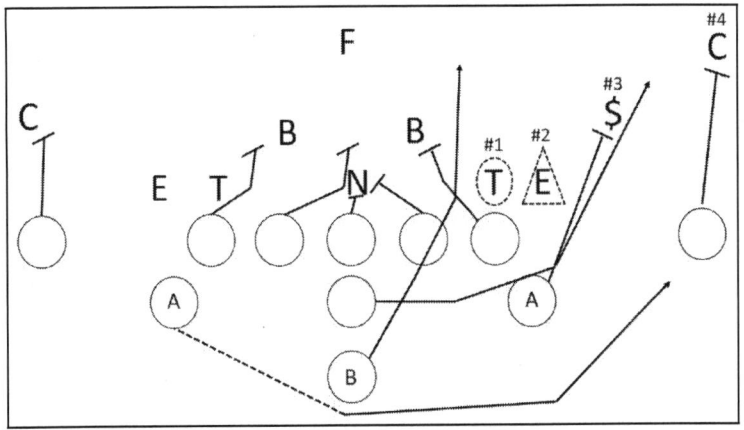

The block of the Wide Receiver is something that is not often emphasized but is hugely important to the big play ability of the Inside Veer. Without a strong receiver core that is able to block and spring the Inside Veer for a touchdown the play loses its power to fully control a game.

Offensive Line

While the heart of the Inside Veer is the Quarterback's ability to read defenders the Offensive Line is the driving force that allows the team to gain yards.

The offensive line for a team that specializes in the Inside Veer does not need to be huge but they must be athletic and willing to fire off of the ball.

Firing off the ball is a crucial element of a flexbone offensive line. This is so important that many flexbone offensive linemen will have a unique stance. Instead of being balanced in their stance and able to move in all four directions, flexbone linemen will have more of their weight going forward. While this can make pulling or getting back in pass protection difficult it allows them to fire off low and get downfield quickly. This is especially important when they are scoop blocking or veer releasing.

The reason why teams run the Inside Veer is in order to help the offensive line. By reading two players the offense is ensuring that they can have a double team on a defensive lineman. When introducing the double team and the importance of blocking defensive linemen it's important to stress to that defensive linemen make tackles for loss and linebackers make tackles for 2-3 yard gains. Because of this the line must make sure they block the defensive linemen first so that the offense can remain on schedule and continue to have the option to both run and pass.

Many offenses rely on strict rules for their offensive linemen to run plays. While these can be a quick way to generate plays it's much more effective when the players know the concept of the play and can work together to make the play successful. The rule for the offensive line is that they are going to double team the first defensive lineman inside of the point of attack. In the Inside Veer the Point of attack is the B gap so they will double team the first player inside of the Guard.

Against a standard Under Front this means the PSG and C will double team any A Gap player. Their goal is to move the player both vertically and horizontally out of the path of the running back. While it is a bonus if they can block a linebacker they should never come off the block to chase a linebacker. Instead they want to move the defensive lineman back and place him in the lap of the linebacker. If they are able to get good vertical movement on the defensive lineman the linebacker will be forced to bow out and go around them instead of attacking downhill. This will cause him to either miss the play, make a tackle for a 4-5 yard gain or attempt an arm tackle that the dive back should run through.

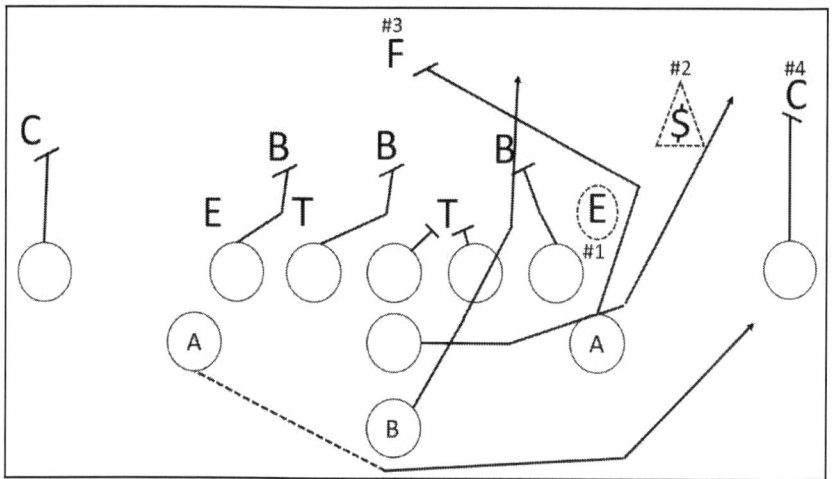

This is an example of Inside Veer vs. a 4-3 Defense. The count starts with the first person outside of the B Gap. This player is #1 and is the dive key (E). The next player stacked behind or outside of him is #2 ($). With this look the PSG and C should double the A gap player to the Backside LB and the Play side Tackle will veer release to the Play side LB.

The Playside Tackle will be responsible for the B gap player. This should be a linebacker who is aligned over the B gap. He will take a Veer release where he will step with his BS foot (in the example above he would step with his Left Foot) at 45 degrees and rip his PS (right) arm through. A coaching point is to tell the Tackles to pick grass as they rip through the defender. This ensures that the dive key can't hold him up and stop him from getting to the B gap defender. Once the Tackle clears the dive key he will climb to the B gap defender and look to pin down his PS shoulder. This, when combined with the PSG and C's double team will create a wall that carries the dive back up to the secondary level.

On the backside of the Inside Veer play the offensive line is executing what is called a scoop block. This is a block that is designed to make sure no one goes across their face. They will take a bucket step and scoop through their play side gap, if no one is in that gap they will continue to climb up to the linebacker level ensuring that no one crosses their face.

The most critical part of the offensive line is that they understand the goal of the play and how their blocks fit into the overall scheme. By using the count system they can quickly identify who the read key is. After they have done this on the play side they should look to control their backside gap. On the backside of the play they are focused on scooping through their play side gap, not letting any players cross their face and climbing to the next level.

Tags

When discussing the Inside Veer many defensive Coaches will stress the importance of playing "assignment football" in order to stop it. The idea of this is that every player has an assignment and if they carry these assignments out they will stop the play. As an offensive coach and play caller it's important to determine how the defense is defending the option by seeing which player is responsible for the Dive, Quarterback and Pitch. Once it's clear how the defense is accounting for each portion of the option tags can exploit their rules and open up big plays.

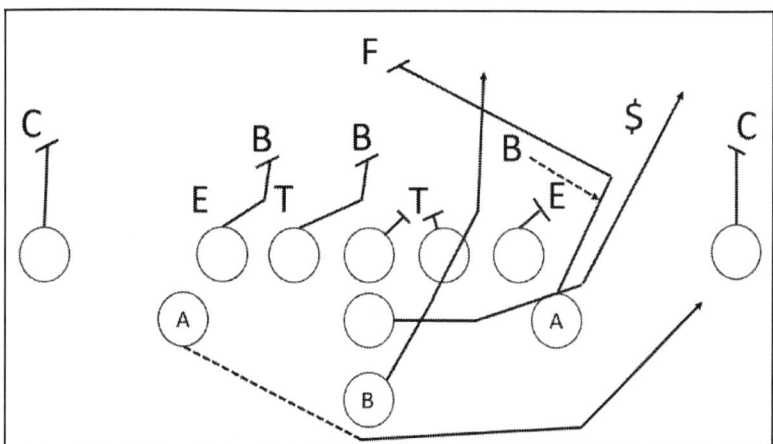

Here is a great example of a time, if the PSLB is scraping over, to use the "Lock" tag

The first tag is used to ensure that you can give the ball to your dive back. Many times defenses will tell the dive key to tackle the dive back every time. They then loop the PSLB outside of the dive key to tackle the QB. This is also referred to as the Scrape-Exchange stunt. This means that the dive back, normally the best runner for the offense, is now eliminated from the play and a linebacker is scraping to the QB.

One way to exploit this is by running Zone Dive where the line will fire out accounting for their play side gap and the QB automatically gives the ball to the Dive Back. An easier way to deal with this stunt this is by running the "Lock" tag. This tag will tell the PST that instead of releasing to the linebacker who is over him he will block the dive key. By blocking the dive key he gives the Quarterback an automatic give read. If the defense is running the scrape exchange now they have looped the Linebacker away from the hole and the dive back has a clear path through the B gap.

The other time the Lock tag can work effectively is when the Dive Key is trying to make the read difficult for the QB. There's a saying that if the defender is easy to read he's hard to block and if he's hard to read he's easy to block. What this means is that if the defender is going to his assignment quickly he may be difficult to block but the QB will be able to read him easily. If the Quarterback is having a hard time reading the dive key though, he isn't moving at the snap of the ball. This makes it much easier for the PST to block him which allows the dive back run with the ball and pick up a gain of 3-5 yards.

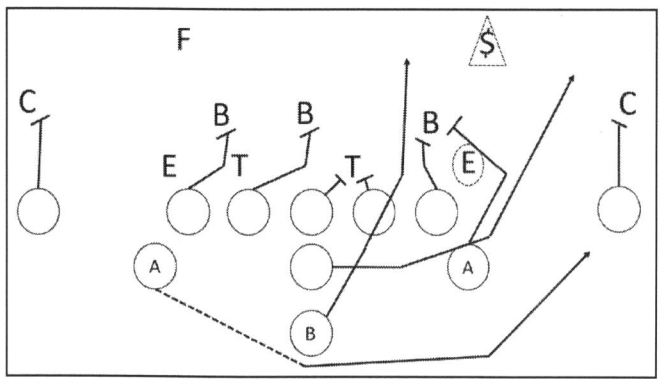

If the PSLB is making plays on the QB it's a great time to use the "Pin" Tag

The second tag is designed to deal with a defense who has a linebacker who is flowing to the QB and Pitchman quickly. Sometimes this can be the result of a scrape exchange stunt while other times the LB is assigned to stop the QB. The Lock tag is a great way to have the FB run the ball on this type of defense but the "Pin" tag allows the QB to get some carries. When the Pin tag is called the play side A is going to block the PSLB instead of releasing into the secondary. While the PST is assigned to the PSLB he will not be able to block him if the LB is flowing quickly to the QB and pitchman. By pining the play the offense ensure that he will be accounted for by having two people assigned to him. If the PS Wing sees that the PST was able to block him he should move on to the Safety.

Tags are a great way to exploit the defense's rules that they have put in place to stop the option. This will cause the defense to get frustrated and start to second guess their assignments which opens the base plays back up.

Play Action from the Inside Veer

One of the best parts of the Inside Veer is that in order for a defense to effectively stop it the secondary must be involved in stopping the run. This opens the door to the big play potential of play action passing.

The general rule for play action passing is that if the defensive secondary is making tackles for less than four yards they are vulnerable to the play action. Obviously this can depend on the players on the field. Some safeties can tackle the pitch back for 3 yards while still ensuring they aren't getting beat deep on a pass.

The play caller should be watching, or have someone assigned to watch, the Play Side Safety. The person watching the safety should be looking for when he comes up to play the run. If he breaks to play the run before the quarterback comes off the mesh he has no chance of defending a play action pass.

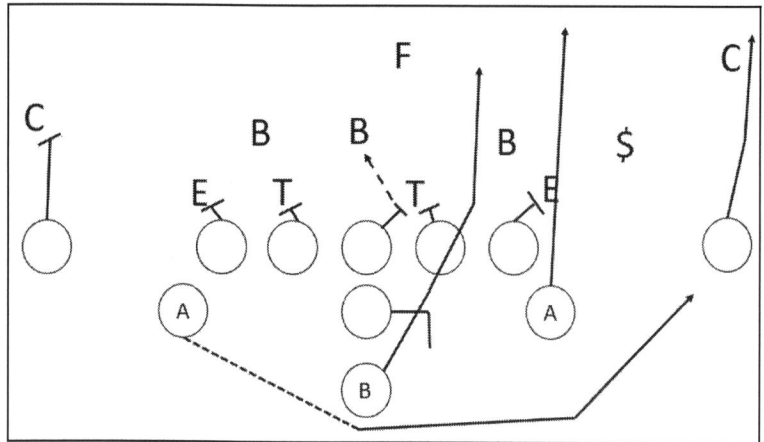

Vs. a 1 High Look the Wing and WR will both run Vertical routes since the CB would be the Near Deep Defender

There are two main play action concepts to run from the Inside Veer. Both of these concepts will put two receivers deep on the play side. The first concept is straight verticals. Here both the PS Wing and PS WR will break off the line like they are going to block the person in front of them. A key coaching point is to have the players look their defender in the eyes, this will make the defender believe that he must get past the block to make a tackle. As the WR and Wing approach the defender they will go past their outside shoulder and accelerate vertically. The play action phase of Inside Veer tends to take a little while, because of this the Slot and WR shouldn't be in a hurry to make their move but instead take their time so they don't outrun the Quarterback's arm.

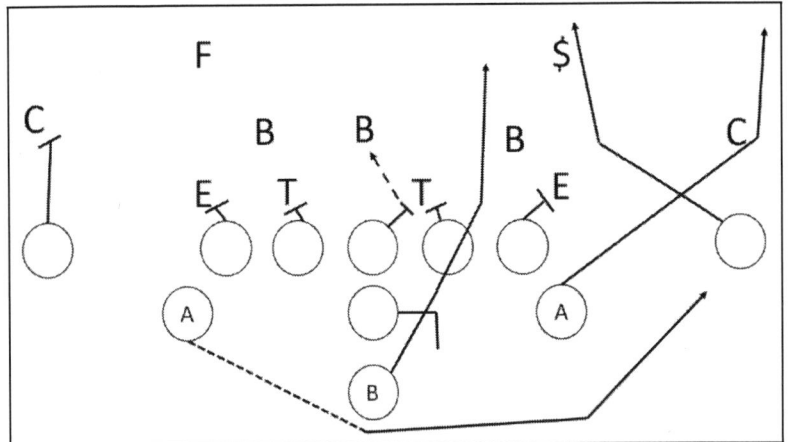

Vs. a Two High look the Wing and WR will run a Switch Route since the WR would be responsible for blocking the Safety who is the Near Deep Defender

The best adjustment off of the Inside Veer Play Action is called the Switch Concept and works especially well against a two high safety look. In this concept the WR will come inside for the Safety like he is going to be blocking him. The Wing will release outside to the Cornerback as if that is his man. Again they will eye the defender to convince them they are going to block them and at the last second escape around them to get vertical. In the switch concept the WR will end up running just inside of the hash marks while the Wing will be running between the numbers and the sideline. Done effectively this can destroy a defensive secondary's reads and create a big play.

With the Inside Veer it's critical to be able to exploit a defensive secondary that is over playing the run. By doing so the play caller is not only creating an explosive play, but also protecting the Inside Veer play and allowing it to run effectively.

Group Drills

One of the universal truths about running the Inside Veer is that it takes millions of reps to master the scheme. The Inside Veer has so many moving parts that the players must work through multiple drills together so each player knows how the other will adjust to what they see. There are a few specific drills that translate to the Inside Veer and allow the offense to master some of the more refined skills.

A Frame

A staple drill of any option offense, especially those that operate under center, is the A Frame Drill. In the A Frame drill the QB, Dive Back and Center can get multiple reps in a very short period of time. The drill gets its name from the lines that are drawn on the field to trace the paths of the Dive Back.

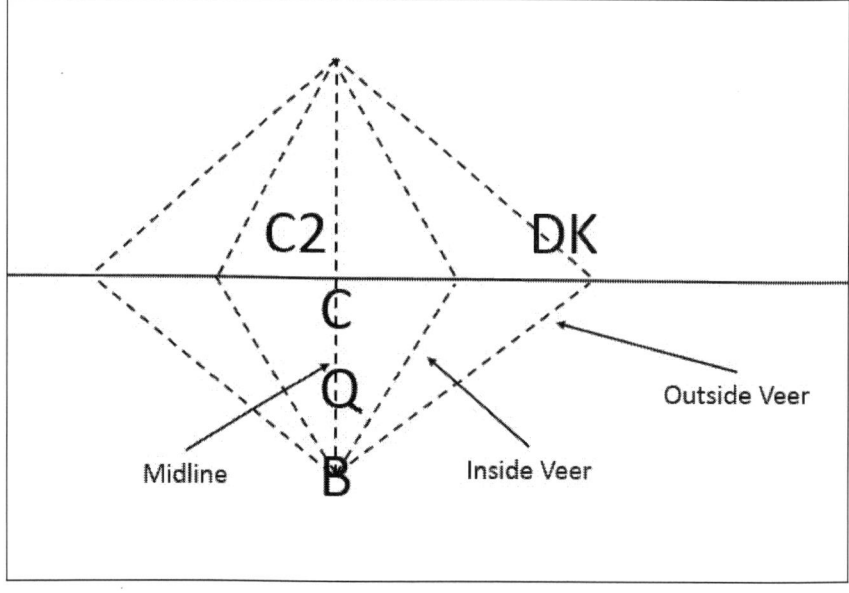

The drill starts with the Center QB and Dive Back all lined up on the ball. The second Center, or Coach, should be acting as an A Gap player and should align how the defense of that week will be lining up. The Coach running the drill should act as the Dive Key and aligns where the opponent's dive key is expected to play. The QB will snap the ball and execute the dive portion of the play while reading the Coach acting as the dive key. This will continue with all of the dive backs and QBs getting reps.

In order to maximize efficiency once all of the players have done it in one direction they turn around and do it back the other way. This decreases the time it takes for the players to line up and allows the coach acting as the dive key to remain on the same side. This saves a small portion of time but because the drill should be run every day the extra reps that are gained everyday by saving these seconds add up over time.

During this drill the Coach is looking to ensure the mesh is taking place perfectly. It's very easy to focus on the footwork of the Quarterback because of the line that represents the path of the B Back when running Midline. Many times the QB who is not currently in the drill can watch the feet of the QB who is doing the drill and give him feedback. This allows the Coach acting as the dive key to focus on other aspects of the mesh. If the offense is doing other option plays the A Frame can be used for every option play.

Mesh

The Mesh Drill is a staple of any backfield that is reading the defense or has complex movements. In the Mesh Drill the full backfield will run the plays without a line. This allows the linemen to specialize and work on their individual blocks while the backfield can make sure their running angles are perfect. Because the backs are working on their aiming points it's important to have some representation of where the lineman and gaps are. The best tool for this is a line hose which has the placement of each lineman laid out. While the line hose is the best, cones placed down to represent the feet of each lineman also serve as good markers.

When drilling the Inside Veer it's important to get many reps reading the dive key. Whichever coach is responsible for the QB and Dive Back mesh should be the coach who gives the read, at least initially. By being the read key the coach can ensure that the QB gets his eyes directly on the dive key at the snap of the ball, this is absolutely critical to the success of the play. The coach who is acting as the dive key should have watched film so he can simulate the alignment and different expected reactions that the opponent will use in the upcoming game.

The next stage of the drill is the pitch read. In an ideal world the pitch key would be a coach as well but if numbers prohibit this it's much better to have the coach as the dive key. In the pitch phase of the play it's important that the QB is attacking downhill and the pitch back is maintaining a good pitch relationship. This can be reinforced by putting a cone on the line of scrimmage about a half yard outside of the tackle and telling the QB he must go inside of the cone.

One variation of the drill is to run it with two balls which is often called (shockingly) Two Ball. In the Two Ball drill the coach who is acting as the dive key is holding a second ball. If the QB gets a give read from the coach, then the second ball is handed to the QB by the dive key and he executes the pitch portion of the play. This can be an effective tool for getting more reps in the pitch phase of the Inside Veer. The downside of this drill is that it's not teaching the QB how to carry out his fake and it doesn't train the QB's eyes to snap directly to the pitch key.

Outside Option

The Outside Option Drill is designed to work the exterior blocking of the Inside Veer. This drill is especially effective at helping players identify the Near Deep Defender and #3 and then teaching them the best angles to take to maximize the effectiveness of their blocks.

In this drill the offense is set up with the WRs and the backfield and they will be going against a Dive Key, a Pitch Key and a Safety and Cornerback. On the snap of the ball the backfield will execute the Inside Veer. The play side Wide Receiver and A Back will need to determine who the Near Deep Defender is and who is #3 and execute their blocks. This drill is also a good time to work with the backs on the best way to use their blocks.

It's critical that the players who are simulating the defensive players have watched film and know the looks and body language that the defense will show during the game. Every defense has indicators that help to show who will be covering the flat and who will be responsible for the deep portion of the field. The coach is responsible for picking these up during film study and then highlighting them for the players during the Outside Option drill.

This is an excellent time to work on the angles that the exterior blockers will need to take to execute their blocks. It's difficult to drill the release a WR must take in order to get to the Playside Safety in time to spring the B Back. In the Outside Option he can get real feedback and work to perfect his job. This drill also helps the ball runners as they can read the exterior blocks and practice using the blocks.

Pods Drill

The offensive line can be tricky to coach with Inside Veer because there are essentially three main blocks that will occur: the scoop block on the backside, the double team on the front side of the play and the veer release. While these skills can vary slightly almost every time the Inside Veer is run players' roles will fall into these three categories. The Pods Drill is a great drill at working these skills with each group of players.

In the Pods Drill the offensive line will be broken up into groups and will work the assignments as a group against the looks they are expected to see in the upcoming game. How they are broken up can vary but essentially the goal is to put players who will be working with each other together. For example if the game plan for the week is to run IV to the side with a 2i and a 5 technique the Center, Guard and Tackle will work together to execute their assignment by doubling the 2i and having the Tackle veer release the PSLB. Once that is done with the right side of the line the coach will turn the other way and have the left side of the line drill the same play vs. the same look. Obviously the coach should mix up the look so that the line is seeing what they expect to see in the coming game.

It's important to also throw some junk fronts where the defense is lined up in weird ways. When combating the Inside Veer some defensive coaches will get crazy with schemes but if the players stick to the count system and understand the concept of the play they will be able to execute the play successfully. Once the front side of the play is worked it's easy to do the same drill but work the backside scoop block. Again the looks should match up to what has been scouted but also include some junk fronts to keep the players prepared.

Made in the USA
Lexington, KY
05 January 2019